CW01267346

THE FORGOTTEN COLLECTOR

THIS IS THE SIXTEENTH OF THE
WALTER NEURATH MEMORIAL LECTURES
WHICH ARE GIVEN ANNUALLY EACH SPRING ON
SUBJECTS REFLECTING THE INTERESTS OF
THE FOUNDER
OF THAMES AND HUDSON

THE DIRECTORS WISH TO EXPRESS
PARTICULAR GRATITUDE TO THE GOVERNORS AND
MASTER OF BIRKBECK COLLEGE
UNIVERSITY OF LONDON
FOR THEIR GRACIOUS SPONSORSHIP OF
THESE LECTURES

THE FORGOTTEN COLLECTOR

AUGUSTUS WOLLASTON FRANKS
OF THE BRITISH MUSEUM

DAVID M. WILSON

THAMES AND HUDSON

© 1984 David M. Wilson

Any copy of this book issued by the publisher as a paperback is sold subject to the condition that it shall not, by way of trade or otherwise, be lent, resold, hired out or otherwise circulated without the publisher's prior consent in any form of binding or cover other than that in which it is published, and without a similar condition including these words being imposed on a subsequent purchaser.
All Rights Reserved. No part of this publication may be reproduced or transmitted in any form or by any means, electronic or mechanical, including photocopy, recording or any other information storage and retrieval system, without permission in writing from the publisher.

Text filmset by Keyspools Ltd, Golborne, Lancs
Printed and bound in Great Britain by Balding & Mansell Ltd, Wisbech

I first met Walter Neurath at the launch of one of his most successful and important series, 'Ancient Peoples and Places': a series which put a new face to archaeology, helped to popularize the subject and made the job of the teacher of archaeology throughout the world immeasurably easier. Few publishers would have had the courage to launch such a massive project; but when he celebrated the twenty-fifth volume in the series he was himself able to appreciate its success. This was but one product of Thames and Hudson inspired by his wisdom and foresight, but one product which made his publishing house the envy of a whole profession. It was, therefore, for me (one of his youngest authors) a great pleasure and honour to be invited to give the lecture which bears his name. He was himself interested in the phenomenon of collecting and connoisseurship and I am sure that the subject of this small book would be near his heart.

1 The only surviving photograph of Augustus Wollaston Franks, taken probably in the late 1860s or early 1870s.

ON 21 MAY 1897 died one of the least-known English collectors, Augustus Wollaston Franks – full of honours in his own lifetime (KCB, FRS, President of the Society of Antiquaries, honorary doctor of both Oxford and Cambridge, member of many foreign academies), but largely forgotten amid the legendary collectors of his period – the Fricks, Morgans, Hertfords, Greenwells and so on. He was a bachelor and his personal heirs were his sisters, nephews and nieces. So there is little family memory, and now alas no personal memory. It is difficult to visualize him, to penetrate his thoughts. Only one picture of him in adult life – a photograph – survives (although the family still possess a portrait of him as a small boy). The portrait on the book-plate used in the books he gave to the Society of Antiquaries is taken from this photograph. The various plaques by Praetorius – the Society of Antiquaries' illustrator – were made after his death, 'executed from very scanty materials'.[1]

When I was appointed to the directorship of the British Museum I had a letter from Dame Joan Evans, daughter of one of his closest friends, Sir John Evans, in which she recalled a visit to Franks before he retired from the British Museum in 1896:

One hardly thinks of Franks as a children's man, but he was very sweet to me and I still cherish a lump of turquoise he gave me which Younghusband had brought back from Leh.

Elsewhere Joan Evans gives a picture of him as a man, the only vignette I have traced:

He was ... a grey dreamy person, with an unexpected dry humour and an incurable habit of addressing himself to his top waistcoat button. These buttons, indeed, served as a barometer of enthusiasm. If he were looking at an antiquity which he liked very much indeed, he fingered the top one; if very much, the next; if moderately, the next and so on down the scale. There were few objects of antiquity which failed to evoke a response of some sort, for his knowledge was incredibly wide.[2]

From his photograph[3] we have a picture of a well-tailored, carefully-dressed, bearded man, perhaps rather valetudinarian (his health is often mentioned in letters and by his friends), with thinning hair and bright eyes. He was a clubman – or at least used the Athenaeum for much of his social life – and he knew people. His friends and acquaintances were legion. When he became a member of the Athenaeum in 1857 (he was 31) he was proposed by the Earl of Enniskillen and Richard Ford and was supported by people as diverse as Sir Henry Rawlinson, Sir Henry Ellis, Octavius Morgan, Felix Slade, Frederic Madden and Lord Stanhope.[4] Through John Evans he came into contact with Sir John Lubbock, Prestwich and presumably Darwin. He knew artists and architects like William Burges, Christopher Dresser, Viollet-le-Duc and Lord Leighton, and practically all the collectors of his generation from the Duke of Northumberland and Lord Hertford to Gladstone, from Albert Way to Henry Christy. He knew and worked together with the great nineteenth-century archaeologists, J.J.A. Worsaae, the dynamic head of the National Museum of Denmark; Oscar Montelius, the man who formulated the theory of typology; General Pitt-Rivers, the wealthy innovator of English excavation technique, and all those who worked together to found the new international anthropological congress. He rarely appears, however, in the memoirs of the period and for any analysis of his personality we depend on his (largely unsorted) letters and his rather arid published work.

Franks was born in Geneva on 20 March 1826 and was christened ten days later in the English Chapel.[5] His father was described in the baptismal register as Captain Frederick Franks RN and was always referred to by his son under this title.[6] In fact Frederick Franks had apparently never progressed beyond the rank of lieutenant, although he had served both in the Mediterranean and in American waters.[7] Frederick Franks married twice, the first time in 1822 to Emily Saunders Sebright,[8] second daughter of Sir John Saunders Sebright. She died in

2 Franks' full armorial book-plate – executed before he received the KCB. By C. W. Sherborn (1891).

E·LIBRIS·AVGVSTI·WOLLASTON·FRANKS
ORD·BAIN·COM·LITT·DOCT·
SOCC·REG·ET·ANT·SOCII·MDCCCXCI·

the year of the marriage.[9] He then married her sister Frederica and, since I can trace no record of the wedding, they may well have married abroad, as (although the marriage was not illegal) within the tables of kindred and affinity it was voidable and considered improper.[10]

Augustus Wollaston Franks was well connected, particularly on his mother's side. His book-plate shows this pride in his ancestry. His Sebright grandfather, the seventh baronet, had married a Croft heiress and Franks' cousin was the 3rd Earl of Harewood. He took his second name from his mother's friend William Hyde Wollaston, a distinguished natural scientist, who was his godfather.[11] On his father's side

9

there was banking money and his great-grandfather, William, had married a Pepys. His grandmother was a Gaussen, a member of a rich Huguenot family; her father was a Governor of the Bank of England and a Director of the East India Company. He had Gaussen relatives in Geneva and it was perhaps for this reason that, after his slightly questionable second marriage, Frederick Franks had settled there.[12] Sometime between 1828 and 1833 the family had moved to Rome, where they were still living in 1841 when their sixth child was born. Late in 1843 Frederick Franks returned to London where he died in the following year.[13] At this time Augustus Wollaston Franks was 18 and on the point of leaving Eton.

In 1845 Franks, following family tradition, went up to Trinity and it is at Cambridge that we get the first glimpse of the clubable and of the antiquarian Franks. Late in life he wrote of his undergraduate days:

Mathematics were in the ascendant, a study for which I had little inclination. My coach (poor Clark of Trinity) said that if I were to devote myself to mathematics exclusively I might take moderate honours for my degree, but that I should have no time for classics, to which I was much attached. Being sure of a sufficient fortune I decided (perhaps unwisely) to confine myself to an ordinary degree, for which I read but a few weeks, and I devoted myself to Church Architecture and Archaeology. I frequented the University and College Libraries, and was one of the founders of the Cambridge Antiquarian [*recte* Architectural] Society, and an early member of the Cambridge Antiquarian Society – of which I am still a member. At the same time I was one of the few undergraduate members of the Ray Club, a very select scientific body of a dozen distinguished persons, such as Sedgwick, Henslow, Clark Babington, G.G. Stokes, etc, and I greatly enjoyed the evenings which each member gave in rotation. The smattering of entomology and botany which I then acquired have been a great pleasure to me through life ... .[14]

1845, the year he went up to Cambridge, was the year of the great row in the Cambridge Camden Society which resulted in the formation of the Ecclesiological Society.[15] Franks as a young member must have been rather bemused by the proceedings. He was clearly much influenced by the Cambridge Camden Society and by the later Architectural Society, for his first publication, which appeared in 1848

3 Plate 97 from Franks' first book: drawing of a medieval glazing quarry in Chassington Church, Surrey.

(although dated 1847), was an account of a palimpsest brass at Burwell. His lifelong interest in genealogy and history is illustrated in an extensive paper on the Freville family and their monuments in Little Shelford church.[16] He graduated in 1849 and in this year published his first book, the famous and well illustrated volume on medieval glazing patterns.[17] The delicate colours of the quarries are well brought out and, although very much the work of a precocious undergraduate, it is still quoted today and shows an awareness of the typological approach which was to colour much of his life.

After Cambridge he moved to London, involved himself in the affairs of the Archaeological Institute and became Honorary Secretary to the Committee for the Medieval Exhibition of 1850, which was held in the rooms of the Royal Society of Arts.[18] It was probably as a result of the success of this exhibition that he was appointed to the British Museum in the wake of the Royal Commission of 1850 which had reported in favour of the establishment of a collection of British Antiquities, against the entrenched views of the Trustees and the Director and under some pressure from the Duke of Northumberland.[19] His account of his appointment is terse and revealing:

In 1851 I was appointed an assistant in the British Museum, with special charge of the British and Medieval collections for which a new room had just been completed. At that time it was thought probable that I should succeed to a very considerable estate and I very well remember the grave consultation as to whether it would not be infra dig. for me to take a post in the Museum, I then being supposed to be studying for the bar. A dear old East Anglian, who was one of my father's trustees, discovered that a Suffolk man (Mr Barnwell) had been employed at the Museum; so it was decided that I might accept the appointment.[20]

Franks was the right man in the right place. The Trustees, while not acknowledging the needs of the Museum with regard to the prehistoric and medieval elements in the collection, had to approve the action of the wily and ancient Keeper of Antiquities, Edward Hawkins, who had set aside a room in the new building for this material and appointed Franks to organize the collections. The early years were not without trouble. Almost immediately Franks crossed swords with the Trustees over a visit to Edinburgh to see a collection[21] and, in late 1857, in a mood of apparent vindictiveness towards Hawkins the Trustees challenged the Society of Antiquaries' election of Franks as its Director,[22] although they had to back down three months later. There was another unpleasantness in July 1857 when Franks, who had done so much to build up the Archaeological Institute, was not allowed special leave to go to the Institute's annual conference at Chester.[23] The Trustees were probably much influenced by the new Director, Anthony Panizzi, who not only disliked his Keeper, Hawkins, but also had little liking for the sort of things that Franks was there to collect, as witness this question and answer to the 1860 Select Committee on the British Museum:

CHAIRMAN: You have, also, I imagine, Byzantine, Oriental, Mexican and Peruvian Antiquities stowed away in the basement? –

Yes, a few of them; and, I may add, that I do not think it any great loss that they are not better placed than they are.[24]

Hawkins, the Keeper, was losing his grip and in some ways sympathized with Panizzi's views. At last, in 1860, in his eightieth year, he retired and his great empire was divided into three, namely Oriental

4 Samuel Birch, Keeper of the Department of Oriental Antiquities, 1860–85.

(that is Egyptian and Assyrian) Antiquities, Greek and Roman Antiquities, and Coins and Medals. A fourth Department, of British and Medieval Antiquities and Ethnography, was adumbrated, but there was not enough money to run it, so it was clumsily lumped together with Oriental Antiquities. Franks, in charge of this cuckoo in the Oriental nest, was allowed a certain measure of autonomy but had to report to the Keeper of Oriental Antiquities, the formidable and learned Dr Samuel Birch. Nothing could have been better for Franks; he respected Birch and soon developed a very warm relationship with him. In the early 1860s Franks had some trouble with his health, which clearly depressed him greatly. In December 1861 he was writing to Birch wondering about resignation. Birch replied robustly:

Indeed you must not think of leaving us as your loss would be really a great one to the department, especially at this moment when questions connected with British Antiquities may arise.[25]

Panizzi was also coming round and was being kind to Franks. Two years later Franks went down with smallpox, but recovered and was much more lively, writing to a colleague:

I am going on very well. My face is diversified with 150 or more excrescences of various shapes which I presume are ornamental as the Doctor says that they are very nice and the Nurse calls them beautiful. As an additional charm the groundwork is of a dusky hue produced by india rubber dissolved in chloroform the exact merits of which I have not yet ascertained. You may break the news to the medal room that I shall probably re-appear with a beard.[26]

Things were coming right for Franks and his Department. Birch was a sympathetic boss and the collections increased. In 1866 the millennium came and Franks became Keeper of his own Department.

By this time he had become a formidable scholar of rather editorial cast. Papers flowed from his pen, he contributed to exhibition catalogues and for some years wrote an annual review of the work of his section of the Museum for the *Archaeological Journal* and later for the *Proceedings of the Society of Antiquaries*. He did not write many books, but they demonstrate the range of his interests; his second book was published in 1858, *Examples of Oriental Art in Glass and Enamel*; his third in 1863 was entitled *Himyaritic Inscriptions from Southern Arabia* and, although it is usually listed under Birch's name, it is clear that Franks did much of the work, particularly the checking of the plates – the proofs of the lithographs, which survive in the Museum, show much detailed correction by Franks.[27]

It is his work on Kemble's *Horae Ferales*,[28] published in the same year, which demonstrates the depth of his scholarship. The book was originally written in German by Kemble (the manuscript survives in the Society of Antiquaries[29]) as a series of lectures to the Niedersächsischer

5 Franks' lifelong interest in heraldry is epitomized by his gift to the British Museum in 1855 of the 16th-century Garter stall-plate of William Parr, Marquis of Northampton. The stall-plate was presumably that removed and defaced when he was deprived of the Garter by Mary in 1553 (he was restored in 1559).

Verein in Hanover. It was translated and edited by R.G. Latham, but the most important part was the compilation, discussion and description of the thirty-four plates which was the work of Franks. This book was the foundation of our knowledge of prehistoric Celtic art. Here is what J.M. de Navarro said about this contribution to this knowledge in his Sir John Rhŷs Memorial Lecture:

Franks's contribution is of outstanding importance: his knowledge of comparable material on the European mainland was greater than Thurnham's; he touched upon problems which still invite discussion, and was the first to envisage the ethnical aspect of the La Tène civilization in its true light. Various reasons led him to regard the objects he described as definitely Celtic, the most cogent being that their distribution is mainly confined to the limits of Celtic occupation and that the patterns on the examples found in Britain differ from those on Danish, Saxon, and Roman antiquities; he notes too that, 'these patterns continued in use among the peculiarly Celtic races of Ireland: though not in a pure state after the introduction of Christianity' – a view still debated to-day. This work of Franks was undoubtedly of greater consequence than any which had yet appeared.[30]

The year before he published *Horae Ferales* he wrote with W.H. Black a paper on the discovery of the will of Hans Holbein; a crucial work, which by establishing the date of the artist's death was the cause of the revision of many attributions.[31]

The breadth of his interests was staggering. The indexes of *The Archaeological Journal, Archaeologia* and the *Proceedings of the Society of Antiquaries*, list subjects as diverse as Indian sculpture, Roman pottery, stone implements, heraldry, seals, ethnographic items, portraits, prints, book-plates, pilgrims' badges, manuscripts, Carolingian ivories, log boats, megalithic monuments in Holland, monumental brasses, chap books, Anglo-Saxon rings, Chinese painting, Amaravati sculpture, and so on. He wrote papers or edited books on oriental porcelain, on the Slade collection of glass, on book-plates, on seventeenth-century tokens, on excavations at Carthage and, with H.A. Grueber, he revised Hawkins' standard work, *Medallic Illustrations of the History of Great Britain and Ireland*,[32] the first edition of which had been withdrawn by the Trustees, who objected for some strange reason to Hawkins' habit of referring to Roman Catholicism as 'popery' and 'romanism'. He completed Lady Charlotte Schreiber's book on playing-cards[33] and wrote a guide to the Christy collection.[34] He did not hesitate to publish on esoteric subjects. In 1868, for example, at the International Congress of Prehistoric Archaeology, he lectured and wrote on the Japanese Stone Age;[35] while six years later at the same Congress (this time in Stockholm) he was lecturing on the chemical analysis of Bronze Age implements from Cyprus.[36] In 1872 he had got involved in the eolith problem, being on the Committee – with Carthaillac, Worsaae and Engelhardt – which examined the Abbé Bourgeois' chipped flints; he was one of the majority who accepted them as artefacts.[37] His status as a prehistoric archaeologist was high and yet, if anything, it was as a medievalist that he had made his reputation and he was also deeply involved with ethnology and heraldry.

It is sometimes difficult to decide whether Franks was an archaeologist or a connoisseur. In the 1860s and 1870s we must see him as the former; indeed, he had an exceptional 'eye' (he was famed for his ready identification of fakes[38]) and, although towards the end of his life he became more of a typical collector of *objets d'art*, one can never see Franks as a dilettante. He seems always to have been in the forefront of the scholarship of his period. One must remember that he was one of the very few professionals in the country. There were many amateurs: Henry Christy, hatter; John Evans, paper-maker; John Lubbock, banker and later Chancellor of the Exchequer; Colonel Lane Fox (later General Pitt-Rivers), soldier; William Greenwell, minor Canon of Durham, and so on. All these people (like Franks) had money, all (with the exception of Lubbock) collected on a fairly grand scale, most of them could give as much time as they wanted to their studies. But Franks was the full-time Museum official. He was also a bachelor and could suit himself as to where and when he travelled or took holidays. He knew all these gentlemen, but he also knew and was in constant contact with his colleagues abroad – with Worsaae, Carthaillac, Lartet, Lindenschmidt, Vilanova, Schliemann, Steenstrup, de Mortillet, Khanikoff, Nilsson and Vogt – most of whom were professionals. He also had

6 Franks sits behind Schliemann as he gives his famous lecture on the finds from Troy at the Society of Antiquaries in 1877. From the *Illustrated London News*.

considerable support from the Museum itself. The Museum Directors of his day were all librarians, consequently the Keepers of the various departments were even more hardened satraps than they are today: Sir Charles Newton, Samuel Birch, Reginald Poole, George Reid. After 1886 Franks was the senior Keeper and as he lived on the premises he was available both in and out of hours to his Museum colleagues and others who cared to see him.

A measure of his professionalism is illustrated by a statement he made towards the end of his keepership:

When I was appointed to the Museum in 1851 the scanty collections into which the department has grown occupied a length of 154 feet of wall cases, and 3 or 4 table cases. The collections now occupy 2250 feet in length, 90 table cases and 31 upright cases, to say nothing of the numerous objects placed over cases or on walls.[39]

As he grew older he was consulted more and more in his official capacity. He was offered and refused (twice) the directorship of the Victoria and Albert Museum (despite the higher salary and proximity of Marlborough House to his Club); he also turned down the directorship of the British Museum. He advised the Swiss government on the site of the Swiss National Museum (his advice was not accepted), he sat on government committees and chaired pressure groups, was an elector to the Slade chair at Oxford and sat on exhibition juries. He was deeply involved in the affairs of the Society of Antiquaries – first as Director, later as President – and of the International Congress of Archaeology and Anthropology, he was Antiquary to the Royal Academy and lived a lively and busy professional life.

*   *   *

I would like now to turn to Franks' keepership and collecting, for in a real fashion he was one of the founders of the British Museum. Within a few months of his arrival he had arranged to purchase twenty-one majolica dishes from the collection of the Abbé Hamilton in Rome, writing about the purchase as follows:

> The numerous collections of Majolica which have been established of late years by the various governments on the continent have so diminished the quality of this ware in the market, that no time should be lost in securing some specimens for the British Museum. The whole of Italy has been so ransacked by foreign dealers that it is useless to expect any number of specimens to be discovered in this country.[40]

This was the start of the Museum's majolica collection. But more important, the way in which the majolica collection was built up is typical of Franks' *modus operandi*. First a modest appeal for a small collection, then cautious buying as pieces of majolica were added to the collection one by one, a vase of the Orsini–Colonna series and a plate from the Pugin Sale. Then came the big push with the dispersal of the Bernal collection. Franks tried to persuade the Trustees to spend £6000 on the Sale, the Trustees asked the Treasury for £4000 and got it.[41] With Cole and Robinson, of what was later to become the Victoria and Albert Museum, Franks creamed the collection, which included a fair amount of majolica. In what was to become a familiar technique Franks laid bait for the Trustees by giving some of his own collection. Writing to Hawkins in March 1855 he says:

> The Museum has recently added several specimens to its collection and is likely to secure still more at the Bernal Sale. I think it therefore advisable to beg the Trustees to accept the accompanying 23 specimens which I have selected as desirable additions to the Museum and superior or different to any in the Bernal collection. They chiefly bear the names or monograms of artists and belong to a class which I am anxious to see collected in the Museum for their great value as documents in the History of art.[42]

After this Franks depended on gifts for the Museum's collections from himself or from friends or acquaintances – in this case a gift from John Henderson in 1878 and a further personal gift in 1885.

7 Majolica roundel acquired by the British Museum through Franks. The inscription records that it was made at Faenza by Baldassare Hanara, 3 July 1536.

8 The Lothar Crystal: the most famous object from the Bernal collection, Franks' first major coup. Probably dating from 865, it was made to the order of Lothar I and depicts the story of Susanna. Frame, 15th-century.

Such a pattern of gradual accumulation, encouragement of benefactions, large purchases and personal gifts was the way Franks set about building the Museum's collections. The Bernal Sale, for example, also provided the Museum with a goodish *tranche* of medieval enamels. This formed the basis of the remarkably rich collection of such material which Franks built on over the next forty years, culminating in his acquisition of the Royal Gold Cup (see below), but including some splendid examples of more 'normal' enamel work like the splendid Mosan plaques he presented in 1884.

9 Enamelled plaque *c*. 1170 representing Samson carrying the Gates of Gaza.

While he was negotiating over the Bernal Sale Franks was at the same time fighting the Trustees over the great collection of London antiquities formed by Charles Roach-Smith, who had himself been very active in drawing attention to the need for a national collection of antiquities when the Trustees failed to buy the Faussett collection of Anglo-Saxon material from Kent in 1853–4.[43] The Roach-Smith collection consisted of some five thousand pieces collected in London building operations in the fifteen years before 1856, together with some foreign comparative material. It took Franks more than a year to persuade the Trustees to purchase the collection. In a remarkably penetrating analysis of it in 1855 he wrote to Edward Hawkins:

> The collection would be a great and valuable addition to the British Room and the acquisition of it by the Museum would go far to remove from us the reproach under which we are labouring of neglecting the antiquities of our own Country, while we accumulate those of other lands. I have had many proofs that such a feeling exists and that it has prevented in several cases donations being made to us.[44]

The trustees were at full stretch with the Bernal Sale, but Roach-Smith lashed about him in print, conversation and letter – even initiated, through Gladstone, a petition to Parliament asking for government money. Franks still backed the purchase (though thinking the collection overpriced) and with the help of Lord Stanhope, a Trustee and a prominent member of the Society of Antiquaries, the purchase was (after some to-ing and fro-ing with the Treasury) completed in March 1856, being checked and registered by Franks over the next three months.[45]

*   *   *

10 Danish flints of the Neolithic and Early Bronze Age, all from the collection of J. J. A. Worsaae, Director of the National Museum of Denmark

25

This was a triumph and it may have been this episode which sparked Franks' interest in the prehistoric areas of the collection. His growing interest in the Society of Antiquaries brought him into contact with the people who were making vast strides in the study of prehistory, particularly with John Evans, whose collecting habits he encouraged, and John Lubbock, the banker who was a friend of Darwin and much involved in the Evolution discussions. It is difficult to sort out the early phases of these friendships. In 1859 Franks went with John Evans to Prestwick's house to view the flints which had been brought back from Abbeville a few days before.[46] He was thus in at the birth of the recognition of the palaeolithic and it seems reasonably clear that Franks was present when Evans read his paper about this material at the Society of Antiquaries. Among the early material of this sort acquired by the British Museum was that from the palaeolithic type-site, La Madeleine itself, given by Christy and Lartet, both friends of Franks. Franks was a serious collector of prehistoric material; omnivorous perhaps, but discriminating. During his time some of the greatest prehistoric collections came to the Museum, influenced undoubtedly by his taste: material from the Swiss lakes, the great Worsaae collection of Danish antiquities, Bronze Age material from Germany, collections from Hallstatt – the gravefield dating to 700–450 BC which is the type-site for the Early Iron Age, visited by Franks in 1876.[47] Also acquired was a substantial group of material from the ritual deposit at La Tène (another type-site), some of it from Franks himself, and Romano–British artefacts, including many of the finest mosaics and much of the everyday material which so clearly reflects the life of Britain at this period.

Franks gave generously of prehistoric objects: a beaker bowl from the Thames, flint-work from Denmark, the Bronze Age founder's hoard from Minster-in-Thanet, and the sheet-bronze shield dating from the period 1200–1000 BC from Rhyd-y-Gorse, the Witham shield with its restrained Iron Age ornament and, amid a large number of finger-rings and so on of Romano-British date, a group of bronzes of which the most important is undoubtedly the famous Hercules, which was probably found near Birdoswald. These are but a few of his gifts in this area.

11 Gilt bronze figure of Hercules from Hadrian's Wall (probably near Birdoswald). 2nd–3rd century.

12 Bronze shield from the River Witham, one of the most splendid British objects of the pre-Roman Iron Age. *c.* 2nd century BC. Originally the bronze was backed by leather on wood. From *Horae Ferales*. Both these objects were presented to the museum by Franks.

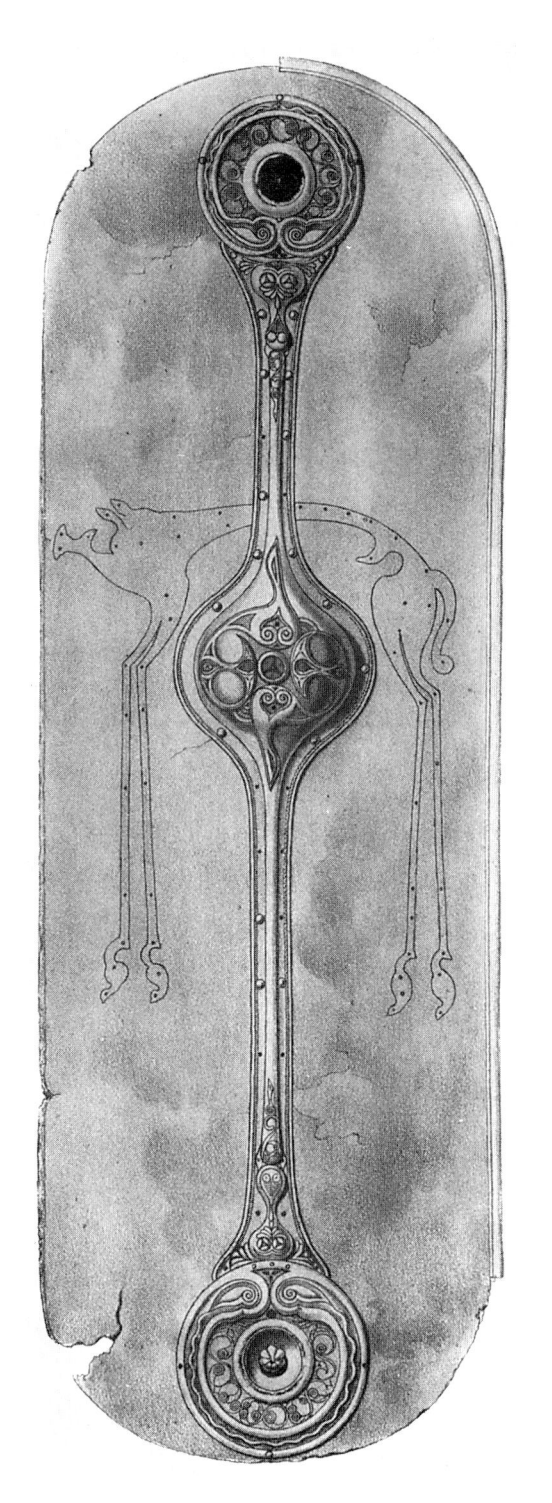

13 Finger-ring of Queen Æthelswith of Mercia (853–88); gold with niello inlay. Inside the bezel is a scratched inscription EATHELSWIÐ REGNA.

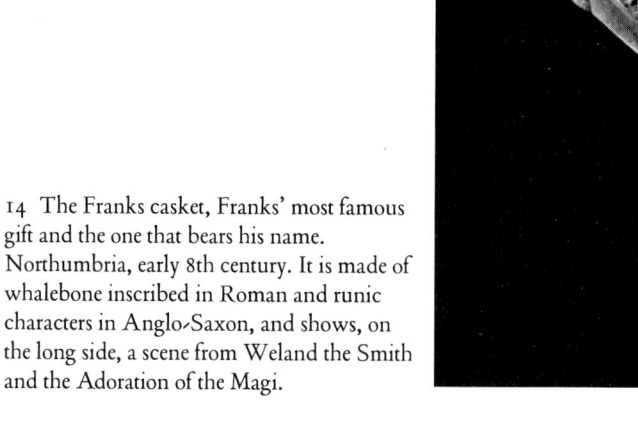

14 The Franks casket, Franks' most famous gift and the one that bears his name. Northumbria, early 8th century. It is made of whalebone inscribed in Roman and runic characters in Anglo-Saxon, and shows, on the long side, a scene from Weland the Smith and the Adoration of the Magi.

29

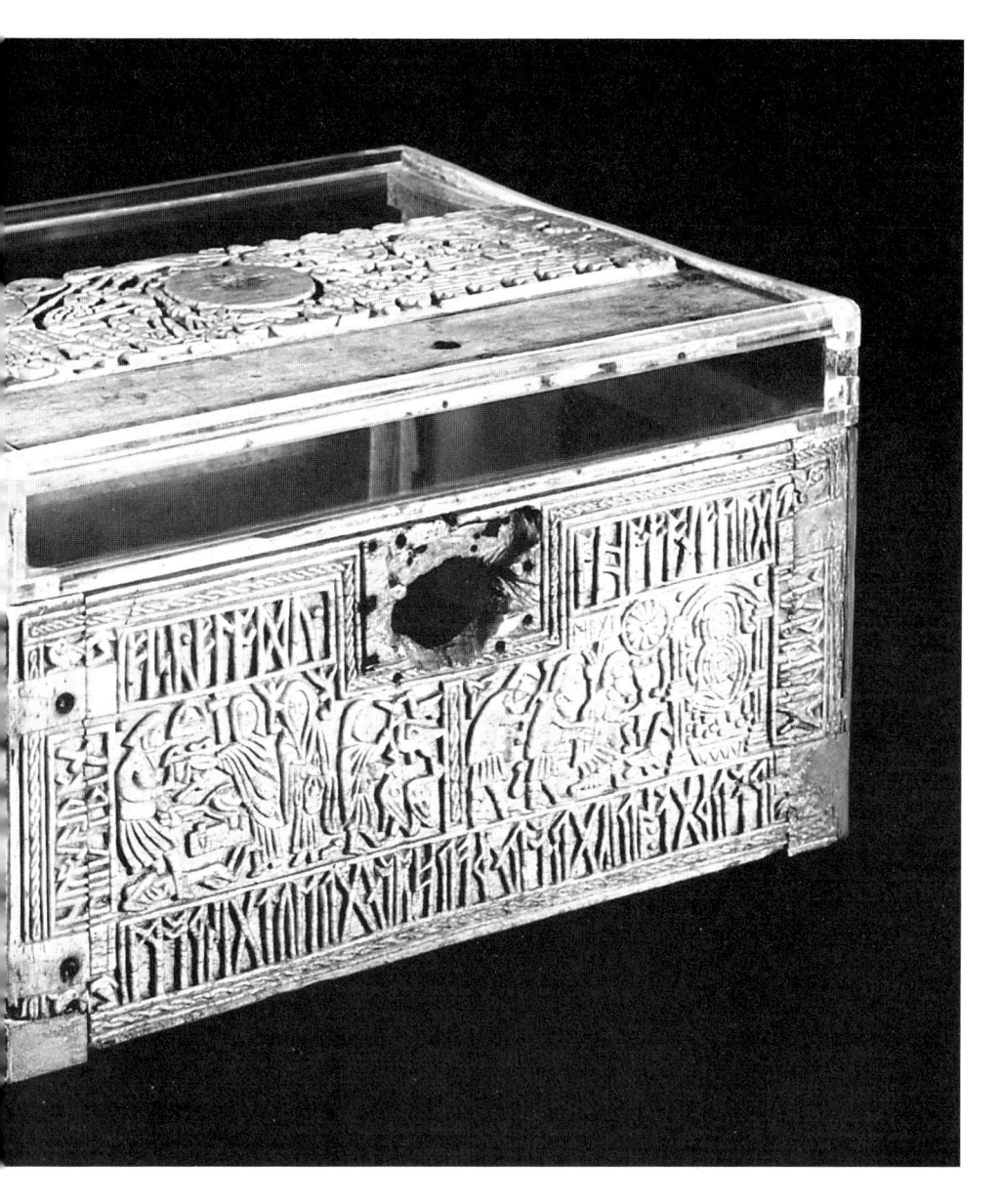

He was no less generous in the post-Roman field. Through his contact with the Anglo-Saxon specialist J.Y. Akerman, Secretary of the Society of Antiquaries, he acquired for the Museum a great deal of cemetery material. But his personal gifts in this field were overshadowed by two important finds – the Franks casket and the ring of Queen Æthelswith. If there is one thing that Franks is remembered by today it is the whalebone box which bears his name. This famous runic-inscribed box was discovered in Auzon in France and sold in Paris. Franks bought it in pieces (indeed one end was missing and is now in the Bargello in Florence). He presented it to the Museum in 1867. The scenes on the casket represent Weland the Smith, the Adoration of the Magi, the story of Romulus and Remus, the Sack of Jerusalem and scenes from a lost Egil story: a strange mixture of universal legend, reflecting the intellectual interests of the Germanic people in a most extraordinary fashion. It was made, presumably in Northumbria, in the eighth century.

The Æthelswith ring, an object made for Alfred's sister (presumably for her to hand out as a gift) in the mid-ninth century, was a collectors' coup of which Franks was particularly proud. It was not, however, an incident without some element of skulduggery. It was found in plough-land between Aberford and Sherburn in West Yorkshire and was said to have been attached by the finder to the collar of his dog. A Yorkshire jeweller sold it to that great collector of archaeological trifles Canon Greenwell, who was a friendly rival of Franks. 'Don't tell this to Franks or Evans', wrote Greenwell, ' for I wish to give them a surprise.'[48] The actual story of Greenwell's acquisition is a rather nice sidelight on the seamier side of collecting in this period, for it had been acquired by the Yorkshire Philosophical Society for the Yorkshire Museum. Greenwell had nobbled the Society, purchasing the ring and promising that he would pass it to the Society on his death. Perhaps as little as three years later he sold it to Franks without consulting the outraged Society.[49]

*   *   *

15 Henry Christy (1810–65), whose bequest in 1865 substantially built up the ethnographical collection. An alabaster medallion by Thomas Woolner RA.

During the period of Franks' career in the British Museum his Department was responsible for the collection of ethnographical material. The first large acquisition of such material was the gift in 1855 by the Admiralty of the Haslar Royal Naval Hospital Collection. From this time forward Franks was hooked on ethnography and in the course of his lifetime gave the Museum more than eight thousand ethnographical pieces drawn from all over the world. 'His purchases and gifts', says

16 Pre-Columbian mask of turquoise mosaic, from Mexico. Donated by Franks.

the present Keeper of Ethnography, 'were not restricted to objects which might have been considered "art" or even to ones showing technical virtuosity: the majority of them were prosaic, utilitarian things which now form the bed-rock of our researches.' He collected more widely than his British contemporaries, Pitt-Rivers and Von Hügel, more akin perhaps to some of his Continental colleagues. In one year, for example 1877, he gave to the Museum stone blades from Ecuador, lip ornaments from Peru, a needle and case from Southern Africa, clubs from New Guinea and Fiji, a Tuareg shield from the Sahara, Eskimo tools from

Greenland, a mask from the Northwest coast, a carved tusk from the Yoruba of Nigeria, dress from Asia and so on.

He was responsible for the purchase of the material collected on Vancouver's voyage to the Pacific and the Northwest coast and for the acquisition of the great Christy collection which in many ways formed the basis of the Museum's ethnographical collections.

Henry Christy, the man who introduced Turkish towelling into England, was some fifteen years older than Franks, but his collecting life – roughly 1850 until his death in 1865 – coincided with Franks' first years at the Museum. In his will he left his French archaeological collections (mainly palaeolithic) equally shared between France and the British Museum. He left his large ethnographical collection and a sum of money to maintain it to four trustees of whom Franks was one. The instructions given in his will obliged the trustees to offer it to an existing institution or to create a new museum. Not surprisingly, then, the British

17 Lid of an ivory salt-cellar, Afro-Portuguese: 16th century. Donated by Franks.

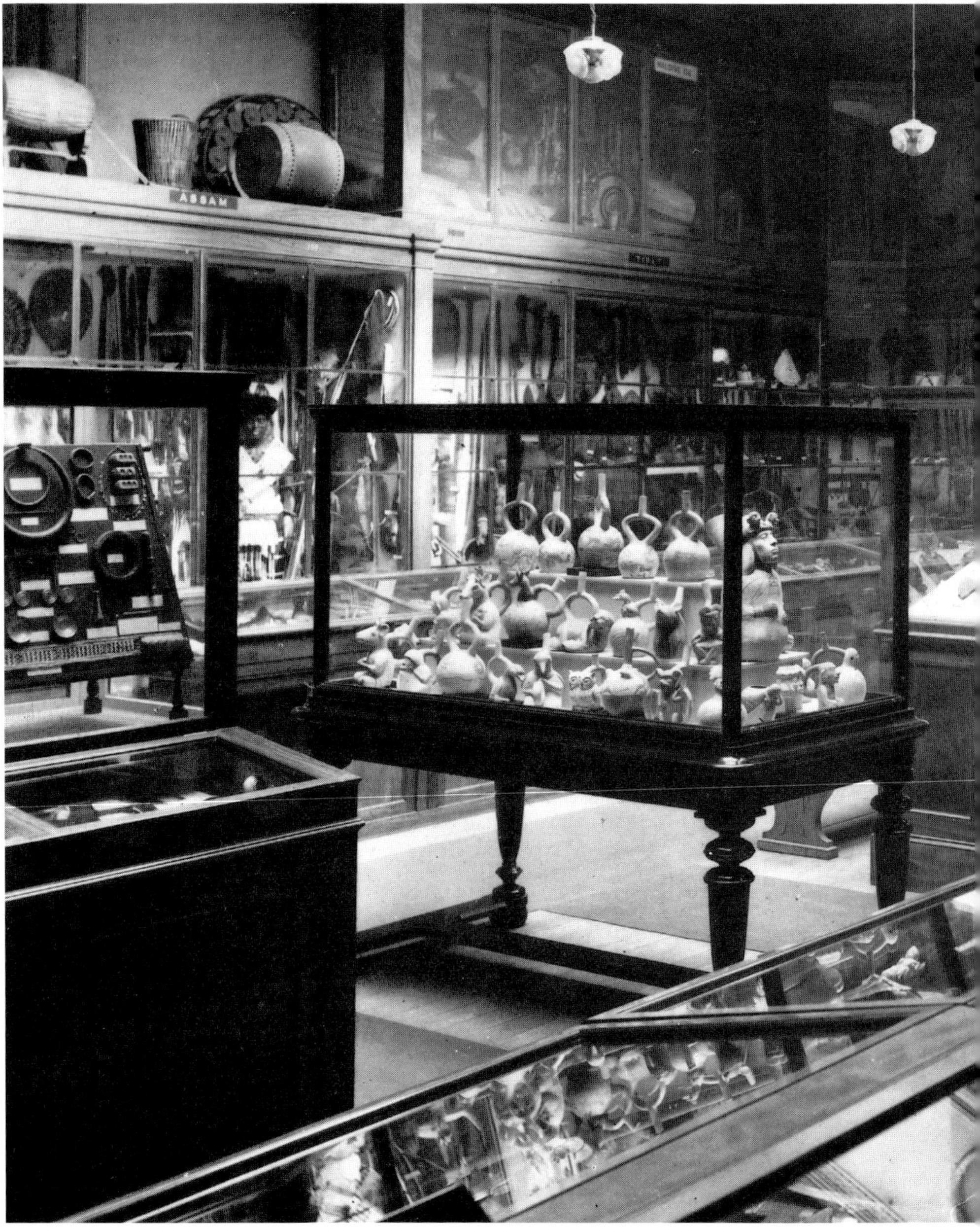
ASSAM

18 The ethnographical galleries towards the end of Franks' keepership.

Museum received its biggest benefaction since its foundation. This in effect formed a separate museum in Victoria Street until 1888, when space was created for it in the Bloomsbury building by the removal of the zoological exhibition to South Kensington. Franks acquired objects for this collection on a very large scale indeed, some through private donors and some by judicious use of the Christy Fund (which, a shadow of its former self, remains to this day). The Christy collection continued to grow and until well into this century was registered separately – all thirty thousand pieces of it.[50]

Franks felt a deep sense of responsibility for the ethnographical collections: he was meticulous in searching out provenances and studying the existing collections and comparative material. He investigated Hans Sloane's collections and his notebooks from his frequent travels contain valuable information about long-dispersed collections. He funded an assistant, Charles Hercules Read, from his own pocket to sort the Christy collection – an assistant who was to succeed him as Keeper. Franks supplemented the library of the Department and employed a draughtsman to draw the specimens in the register. We should remember that it is largely due to Franks' work that Britain now has one of the finest collections of ethnographica in the world. This is what he himself wrote of it:

> ... a collection of considerable size one of the best in Europe, and such as ought to be in the National Museum of a country like England ... From my coming to the Musuem to the present time [c. 1896] the whole amount that has been expended on the collection does not exceed £1800 of which £1000 has been devoted to American antiquities ... It is probable that my own contribution in gifts or expenses including those which I have made to the American and Asiatic sections, is not less than £5000.[51]

Among his many donations were three of the pre-Columbian turquoise masks and much of the splendid collection of Afro-Portuguese ivories which were exhibited in 1982/3. But he also collected more scientific specimens – Asante fetishes, for example, very unimpressive to look at (a few fish vertebrae, a twist of fibre, etc.) but of great scholarly interest.

19 Priest in meditation, made in Japan before 1600: one of Franks' most important gifts of oriental art.

20 Porcelain ewer decorated in underglaze blue. Chinese, 15th century.

We have seen that Franks was interested in Asia and here again he made pioneering collections. He corresponded with Stephen Bushell, one of the pioneers of the study of Chinese ceramics, then at the British legation in Peking, and formed a large collection of Chinese porcelain which according to modern specialists reflects an understanding of the subject far beyond that of most of his contemporaries. The pottery he gave to the Museum ranges in date from the fourteenth to the nineteenth centuries; not merely the fashionable export wares, but also Ming monochrome and polychrome enamelled wares, and even fourteenth- and fifteenth-century underglaze blue wares. His collection of Japanese pottery and porcelain was less eclectic, but he acquired hundreds of pieces at the Paris Exhibition of 1878, which are now particularly valuable as they reflect the Japanese export market of the time. His oriental ceramics were displayed in the Bethnal Green Museum for some years and Franks, naturally, wrote a catalogue on the subject. He acquired many Japanese pieces of an archaeological nature, including the Museum's only example of a complete Haniwa figure of the Great Tombs period. He also ventured into the decorative arts and amongst the most important of his gifts was the famous figure of a priest in meditation which dates from the sixteenth century.

Although he gave little Indian material it was through his efforts that the British Museum's incomparable Indian collections were founded. He acquired the Amaravati sculptures from the India Museum and he personally negotiated the gift of the remarkable Bridge/Stuart collection of two hundred pieces of Indian sculpture collected between 1777 and 1828 by General Charles Stuart (Hindoo Stuart). Having first purchased it 'for a song', the Bridge family were then persuaded by Franks to give it to the Museum if the Museum paid transport costs. Here, however, he had little expertise, was little interested in provenance and merely bought within his taste. He did however collect Iznik pottery with great scholarship and expertise, and his collection and that of his friend Frederick Godman which came to the Museum in 1983 help make the Museum's holdings in this area the best in the world.

21 Iznik covered bowl, between 1560 and 1580.

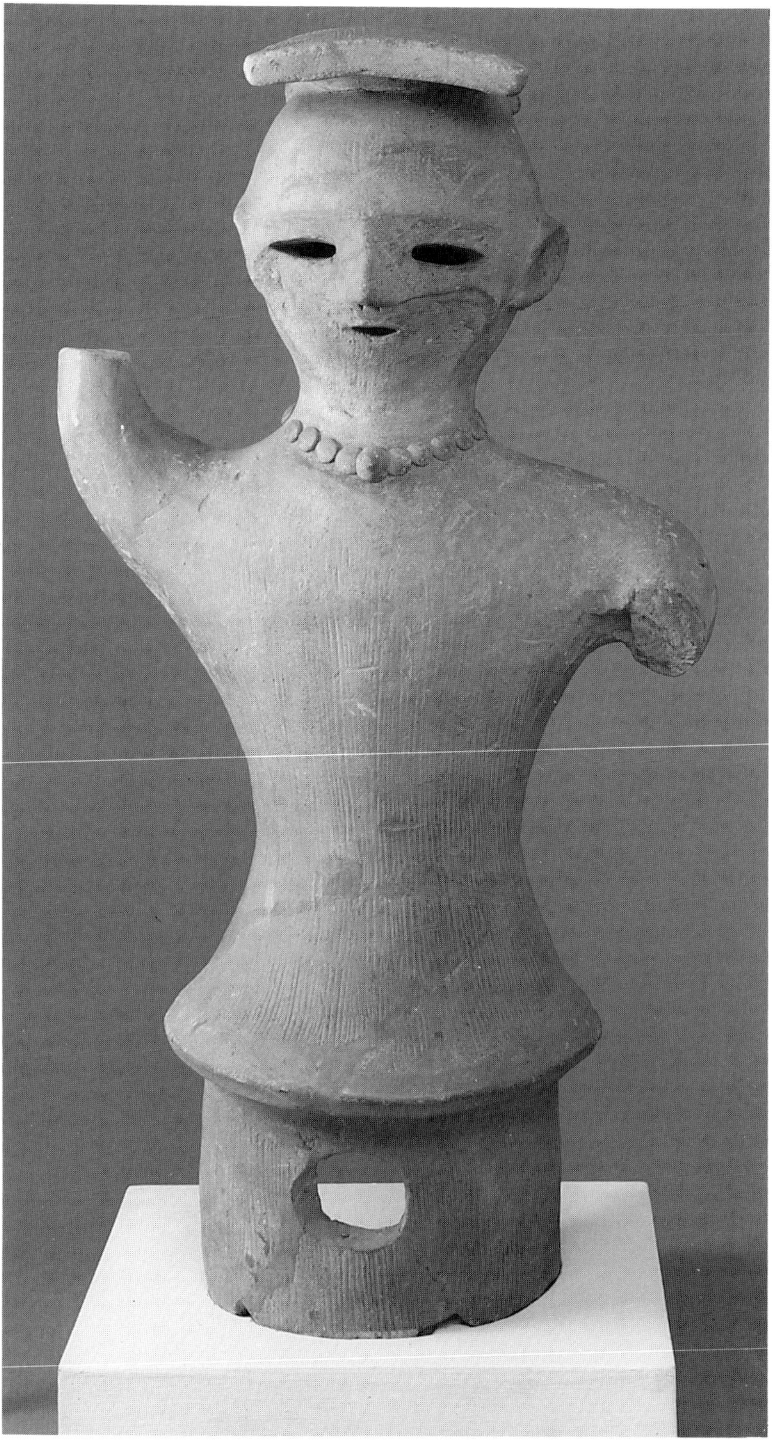

Franks was a European – he had been brought up on the Continent, he travelled widely in Europe, he had numerous friends there, he spoke the languages and he knew its history. For this reason his collecting enthusiasm was based eventually on European history, and particularly on the medieval period. Of this field he wrote:

The medieval collections have chiefly grown by gift or bequest ... The three principal bequests have come from my own personal and intimate friends, whom I had helped in forming their collections. These were Mr Slade, Mr Henderson and Mr Octavius Morgan. To the first two I was an executor and Mr Morgan consulted me specially as to his bequests. The other principal bequests, but not as extensive, were from friends of mine, Lady Fellows and Mr William Burges. The gift of the remainder of the Meyrick Collection was due to General Meyrick's knowing that I had recommended strongly to Government the purchase of the Meyrick Collection ... I have been able to add a great number of specimens of all kinds and sorts.[52]

His proudest acquisition, however, was undoubtedly the famous Royal Gold Cup of the kings of France and England, a cup of solid gold embellished with translucent enamels with scenes of the Life of St Agnes, given in 1391 to Charles VI of France by the Duc de Berry. It is a secular cup and one of the few surviving pieces of medieval royal gold plate. Franks tells the story of its acquisition best:

I had known it for some years in the possession of Baron Pichon, who asked for it the hopeless sum of £20,000. When however I found that it was actually in this country, I persuaded Messrs Wertheimer, the new owners, to send it to me for examination ... Seeing the inestimable value of the object as an historical relic, and as a work of art, I agreed with Messrs Wertheimer for the purchase. They very generously ceded it to me at the cost price to them [£8000] ... For some time I could not make up my mind whether I should take the purchase on my own shoulders, or allow others to help me. Reflecting however that if I bought it myself and gave it to the Museum with my other objects of a like nature, it would dwarf my own examples of the kind, and that my purchasing powers would be curtailed for a long time to come I decided to try and raise a subscription as suggested by Mr Fortnum, in which I have been fairly successful. The present deficiency for which I am responsible being under £1000.[53]

22 Pottery Haniwa in the form of a woman. Japan, 5th–6th century AD.

23 Carolingian covered cup of unknown provenance. Silver and niello.

But the bequest of plate which the Museum received[54] does not really pale into insignificance beside the Royal Gold Cup. Ninety-nine pieces of silver and gilt plate of all periods from the Carolingian to the eighteenth century form the core of the British Museum's collection of European plate, which includes some heirlooms of his mother's family, the Sebrights (purchased in the Sebright Sale in 1887), and an

24 Lid of the cup shown opposite.

important group of English mazers. He also bequeathed to the Museum his vast collection of finger-rings of all periods[55] and other objects galore.

It would be difficult to enumerate all his gifts to the Museum, his European pottery, porcelain and glass, scientific instruments, oriental manuscripts, Egyptian antiquities, medals, his Battersea enamels, the

25 The Royal Gold Cup of the Kings of France and England. Franks' greatest purchase, for which he raised £8000 in private subscriptions.

'Treasure of the Oxus',[56] and the collection of eighty thousand bookplates.[57] Everywhere one turns in the British Museum his name appears as the donor on labels. His great bequest of 3330 pieces crowned a lifetime of generosity without parallel in the history of the Museum. At the same time his responsibility for purchases reflects his taste and the breadth of his vision. The roll-call of great collections taken into his care is impressive, the Roach-Smith collection, the remnants of the Fountaine, Bernal, Meyrick and Blacas collections, Morgan, Worsaae, Slade, Fellows, Bähr, Burges, Schreiber, the Indian Museum and, above all, Christy. But there were also small collections, smaller acquisitions given by friends or purchased by acquaintances and bequeathed to the Museum. On 24 May 1880, the dying John Jope Rogers wrote from Helston:

> I send you ... the little find of Anglo-Saxon silver and bronze ornaments found at Trewhiddle, in Cornwall, in 1774 ... Kindly present these to the Trustees of your Museum as a small token of my regard for you, as the benefactor to so many branches of the National Collection over which you preside ...[58]

The acquisition of this vital Anglo-Saxon hoard, which contains not only important ornamented strips, but also the earliest English chalice, was typical of much of Franks' boundless friendship and enthusiasm.

*   *   *

The following pages represent a cross-section of objects acquired by the Museum under Franks, all but fig. 28 given by him.

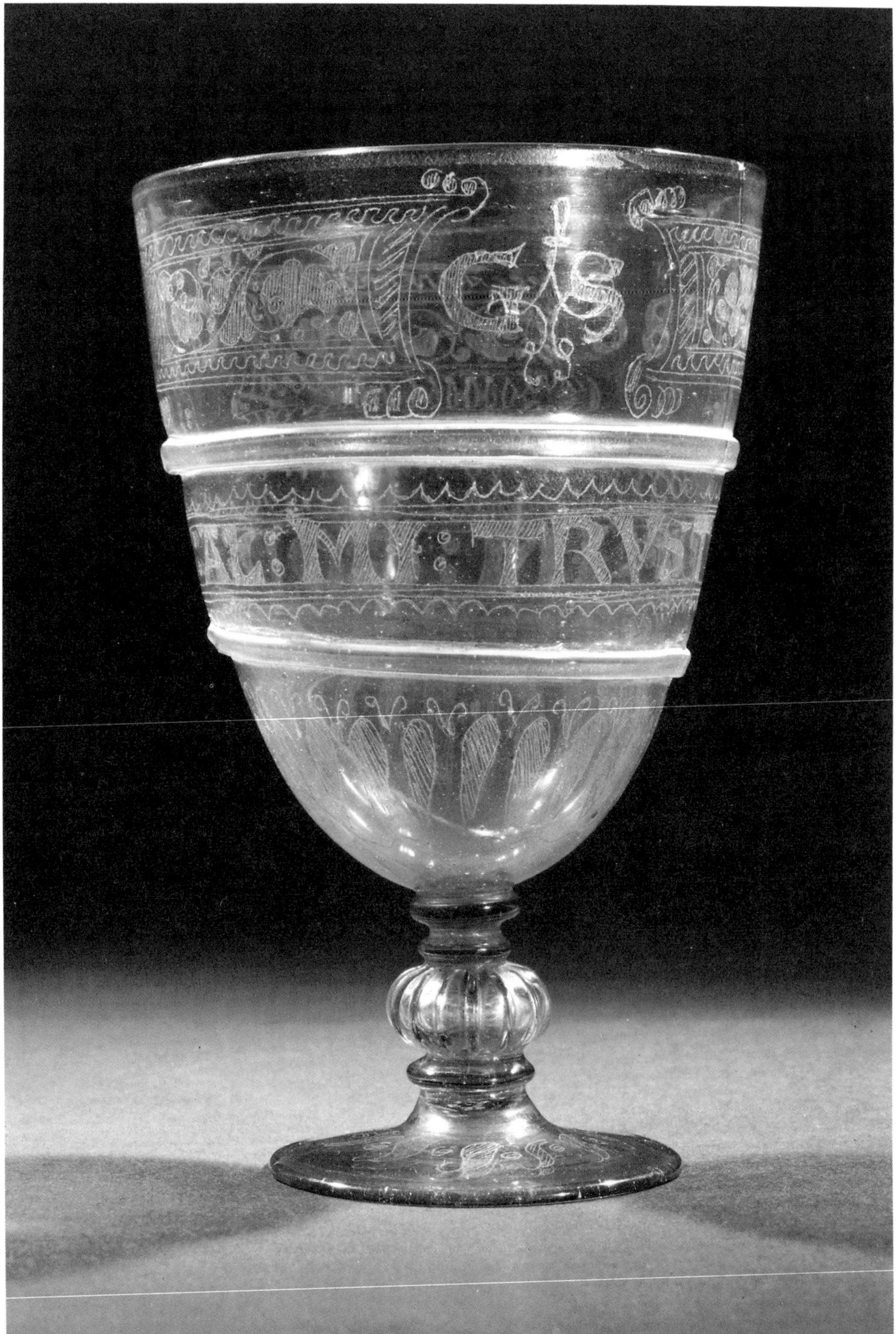

26 Through his friendship with Felix Slade, Franks acquired for the British Museum the large Slade collection of glass. In 1895 Franks gave this English glass, dated 1586 and attributed to Jacopo Verzelini.

27 Horizontal inclining dial made for William, sixth Lord Paget, by Thomas Tompion, London 1703, the only known solid gold scientific instrument.

28 Gold 'lion griffin' from the 'Treasure of the Oxus'. Probably Scythian 4th–3rd century BC.

29 Silver parcel-gilt rhyton. Achaemenian 5th century BC, from Enzincan, N.E. Turkey.

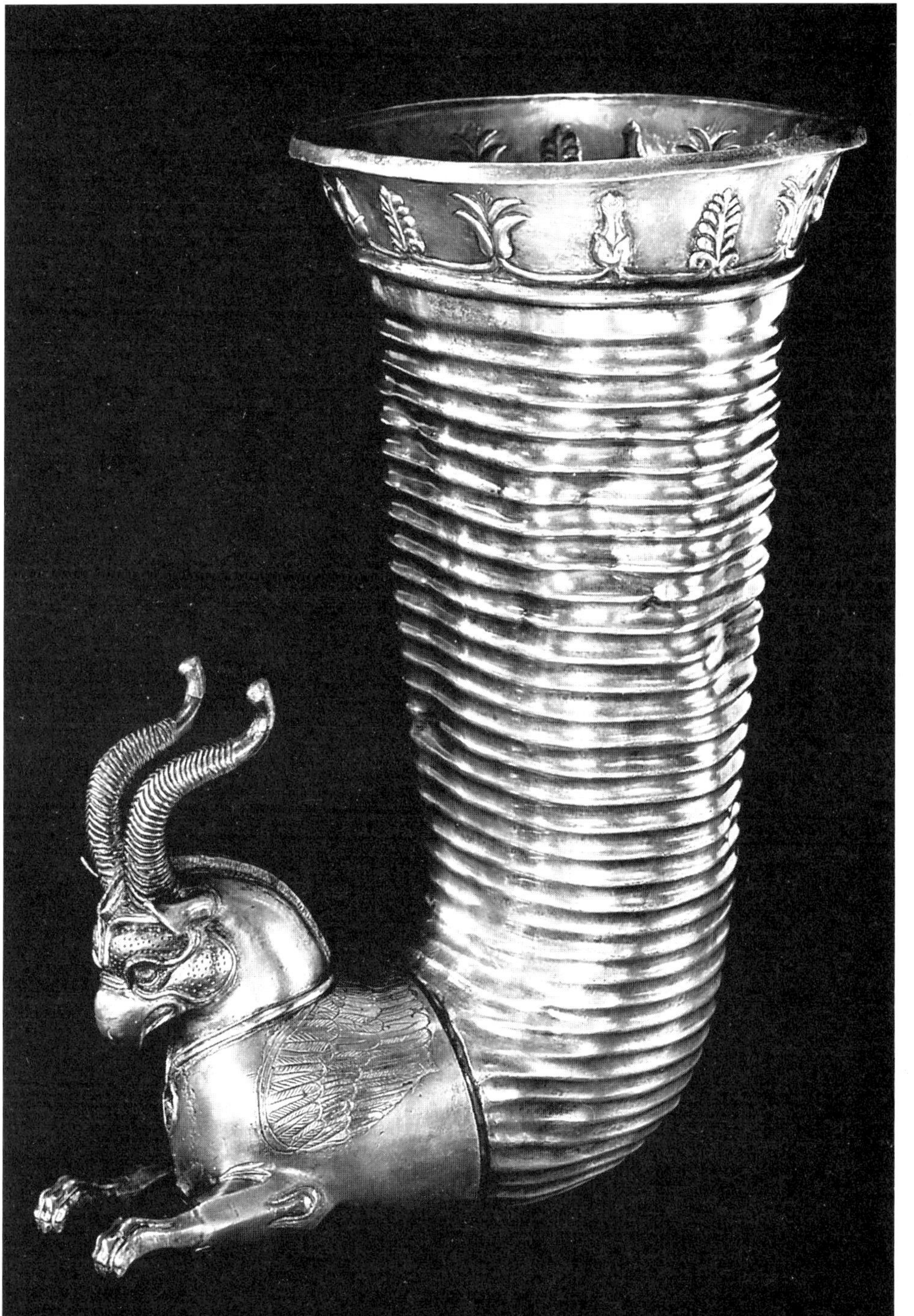

50

31 Franks' interest in pottery and porcelain was remarkably broad. Wherever possible he bought documented pieces. This is a Meissen cup by C. F. Herold, dated 1750.

30 Jug and cover of soft-paste porcelain moulded with strawberry leaves, Chelsea 1745–9. The cover does not match.

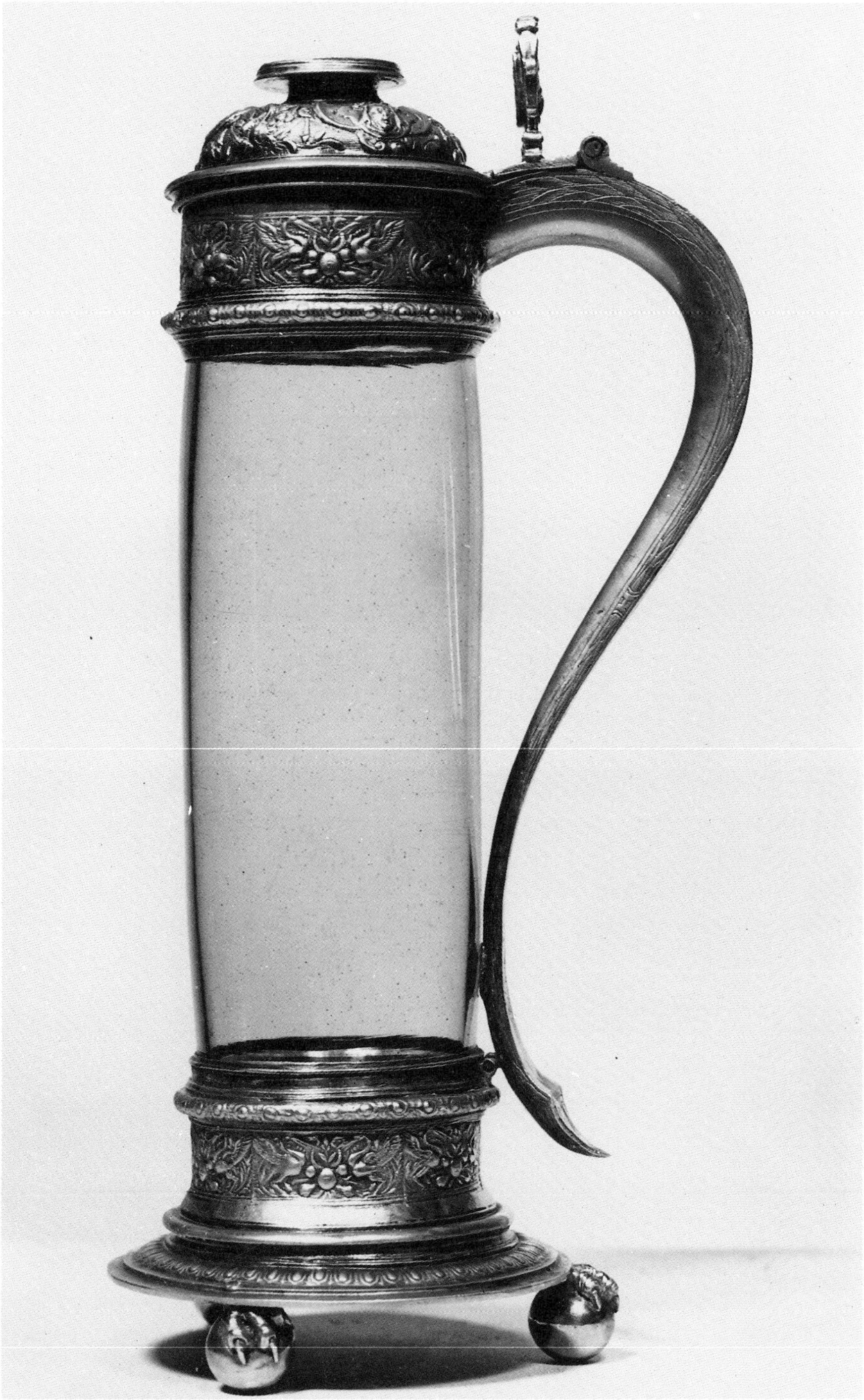

33 Medal depicting John Kendal. Struck in 1480, the year in which Kendal was appointed Grand Prior of the Order of St John of Jerusalem in England, this is the first contemporary medallic portrait of an Englishman.

34 Medal by Nicholas Briot celebrating Charles I's return to London after his Scottish coronation.

He also helped other institutions. He gave a couple of paintings to the National Gallery, of which the Philippe de Champaigne triple portrait of Cardinal Richelieu is the most famous. He steered books to University College London, and advised Lady Charlotte Schreiber on the disposal of her various collections between the Victoria and Albert Museum and the British Museum. His vast collection of brass-rubbings (some three thousand of them) and many of his books went to the Society of Antiquaries. He reported on the Petrie collection, which became the core of the National Museum in Dublin. His energy was astounding, his correspondence voluminous and his social life extensive. But he remains an enigmatic person. How, for example, did he manage the logistics of collecting? It was easy enough with book-plates, they could be sent by post and exchanges were arranged with other leading

32 The Burleigh Tankard, a glass tankard with enamelled silver-gilt mounts bearing the arms of the first Lord Burleigh. Probably made 1572–5.

35 Triple portrait of Cardinal Richelieu by Philippe de Champaigne, given by Franks to the National Gallery, London.

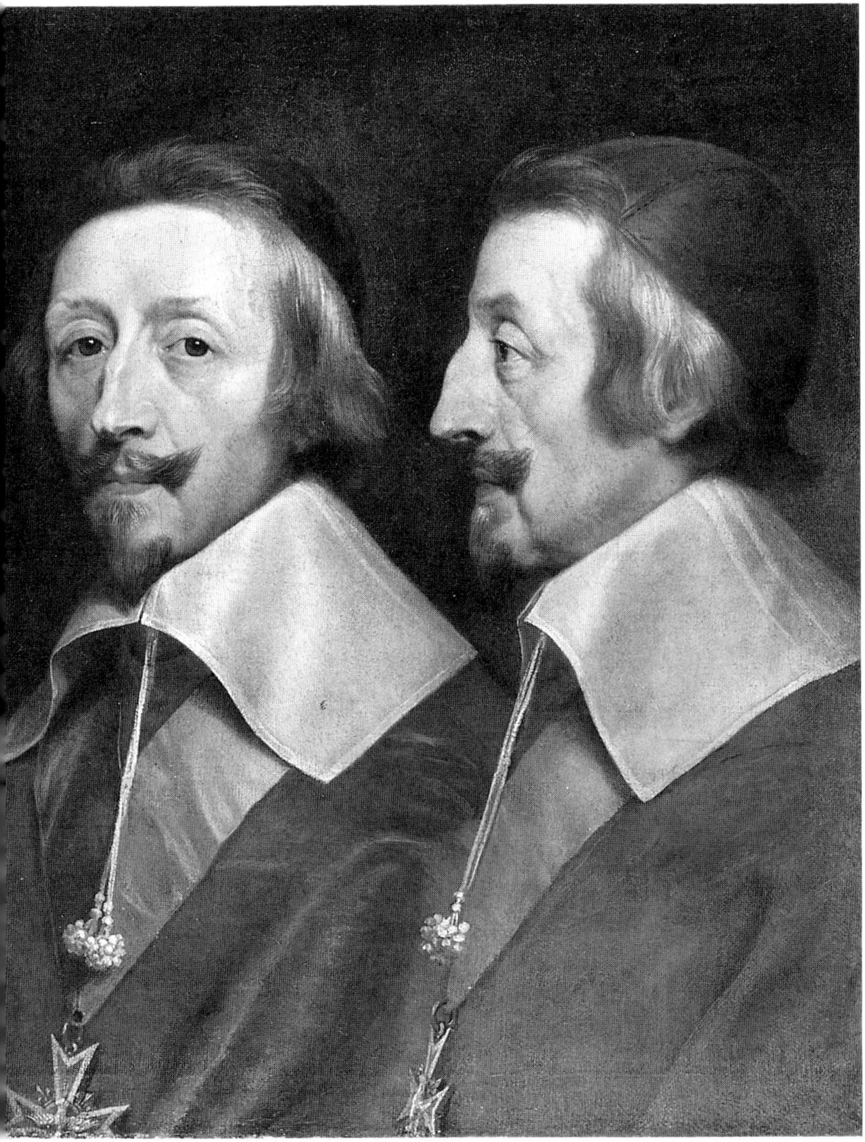

collectors on a gentlemanly basis, big collections, the Bilco and Rozière collections for example, were purchased *en bloc* and the collection of Lord de Tabley – a lifelong friend – passed into his hands in 1895. But collecting pottery and porcelain was not quite so easy. Such material had to be packed and transported to London, unpacked and arranged in one of his houses. He bought all over Europe, particularly in Paris, but the dealers he used are practically unknown. Whilst he was careful to record archaeological provenance his records of purchases do not survive, but this may be because his executor, Charles Hercules Read, destroyed them. Material of the sort he collected was going reasonably cheaply at this period, the age before Pierpont Morgan, Schnütgen and Hearst. He did not collect pictures or furniture, all very expensive at this time, and he did not pursue classical or Mediterranean antiquities, which were being collected by his colleagues elsewhere in the Museum. His most

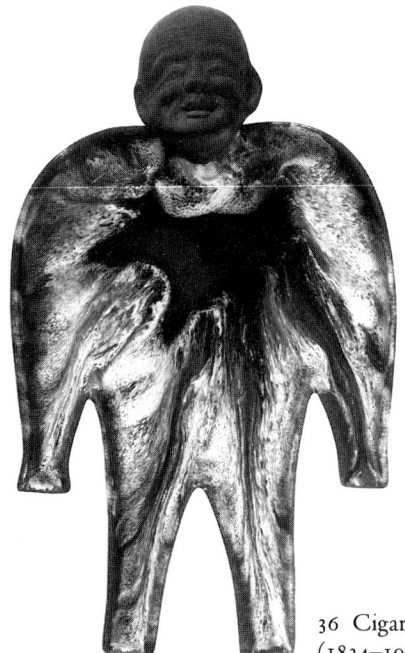

36 Cigar tray by Christopher Dresser (1834–1904).

37 Gold jetton (most copies were made in silver) struck by Franks for presentation to friends.

expensive collecting was in the area of silver and gold plate, but he made killings in finger-rings and jewellery (portable material which could be picked up in dealers' trays all over Europe and transported easily). He occasionally collected newly manufactured material. It was Franks, for example, who left to the Museum a pretty hideous cigar tray by Christopher Dresser – the first article by this designer to be incorporated into any public collection – for such objects he presumably paid market prices.

It is to be noticed that Franks never collected on his own behalf medieval or later sculpture, stained glass (although I have a suspicion that his collection of this material was intended for the British Museum and got away in the Hercules Read Sale) or western furniture. This may well have been through lack of space. He didn't live in a castle – like Burrell or Astor for instance – or in a large house, like Ferdinand Rothschild. For the same reason he apparently had few pictures (his father's large collection was sold),[59] although he hung on to some family portraits which were left to his sister. He was a hard bargainer and had a very real knowledge of the market, thus occasionally missing items because of what he considered to be inflated prices. He had only a modest fortune and could not afford the really fashionable material, Renaissance plate and jewellery, for example, although he may have influenced Baron Ferdinand Rothschild's large bequest of this material to the Museum (it came in 1898, the year after Franks' death). He also avoided large virtuoso works of continental porcelain.

38 A number of Franks' sketch-books survive. This page shows a drawing made in Malines of the 8th-century Anglo-Saxon Genoels–Elderen plaque.

His archaeological collections were acquired at little cost, were sometimes given to him or sometimes exchanged (as, for example, with Sven Nilsson of Lund[60]). As for the ethnographic material, this was picked up extremely cheaply at this period. Like all good collectors he looked for unfashionable material and bought in bulk.

As for the man himself, although obviously a very public man, it is difficult to gain any view of his private life or habits. He was clearly a rather conservative character – I suspect he was Conservative in politics. That he had a proper sense of his own importance is demonstrated by a medal he had struck for presentation to his friends. He moved at a fairly high level of society, but unusually for the period he also moved among the high academics of Europe. He was a good linguist and travelled easily and often, but never seems to have adventured outside Europe. He was unknown (apparently) to American collectors. He visited an amazing number of European museums and his notebooks with their

39 Franks' grave-slab in Kensal Green cemetery.

splendid sketches attest both the catholicity of his taste, the accuracy of his scholarship and his attention to detail. He had a dry sense of humour and was keenly interested in money. Unmarried, he was supportive of his family – of his mother until she died and of his sisters. He was loyal and devoted to the British Museum; he was delighted to be made a member of the Standing Committee of the Trustees after his retirement. His memorial lies in the four departments of the British Museum – Ethnography, Oriental Antiquities, Prehistoric and Romano-British Antiquities and the core of his old department, Medieval and Later Antiquities – which he created. Outside the Museum he may be forgotten but his memorial can be seen in the National Art-Collections Fund, one element of which was founded as a direct result of his death.[61] Typical of the many ways his reputation has benefited scholarship is the fact that it was a Franks' memorial studentship that started Sir Mortimer Wheeler on his career in archaeology.[62]

Franks was buried in Kensal Green Cemetery, amid all the worthies of West London's Victorian era, under a decorous tomb-slab of red granite, bearing a floreated cross in relief, within twenty yards of the mausoleum of the founder of Birkbeck College. As I cleared the undergrowth from his tomb in the autumn of 1983 it seemed almost symbolic of Franks' reputation: only now are we beginning to understand the extent of his generosity and of his genius. Few people nowadays have heard of him and very few have kept his memory green. I trust that this short essay will help in some measure to bring him once again the recognition he deserves, a recognition which was his a hundred years ago but one which has been hidden partly because of the breadth of that genius.

NOTES

1. *Proceedings of the Society of Antiquaries of London* 1897–9, 154.
2. J. Evans, *Time and Chance* ..., London 1943, 143.
3. I am deeply indebted to Dr D. Roe for allowing me to reproduce the photograph of Franks. For the circumstances of its discovery see *Antiquity* lvi (1982), 1. It was probably taken in the 1860s or 70s.
4. Athenaeum election book.
5. London, Guildhall Library: *Register of Baptisms ... belonging to the English Chapel Geneva 1820.*
6. E.g. in his *Who's Who* entries.
7. Wright family MSS.
8. Hertfordshire Record Office: Flamsted Marriage Register, 30 March 1822. It is not without interest that her marriage is suppressed in Burke. Her name does not appear at all in modern editions.
9. *The Gentleman's Magazine* xcii (July–Dec. 1822), 478.
10. *First Report of the Commissioners ... to Inquire into the State and Operation of the Law of Marriage as relating to the Prohibited Degrees of Affinity ...*, London 1848, 237.
11. An Augustus Wollaston of Whitehall was a trustee of his great-grandmother's (Mary Pepys) marriage settlement (A.C.C. Gaussen, *A Later Pepys*, London 1904, 22), but he can only have been a distant relative of his mother's friend William Wollaston. Franks seems to have been known by the name 'Wollaston' and rarely – at least in his later years – as 'Augustus'.
12. For the Gaussen connection see ibid. and A. Gaussen, *Men of the Midi*, London 1934.
13. *The Gentleman's Magazine*, Jan.–June 1844 (8 May).
14. 'The Apology of my life', by AWF. Wright family MS. This unpublished memorandum (referred to here as *Apology*) was apparently seen by C.H. Read who used it in writing the *DNB* entry on Franks. I am grateful to Miss Wright for allowing me to quote it freely.
15. J.F. White, *The Cambridge Movement*, Cambridge 1962, 153.
16. A.W. Franks, 'On palimpsest sepulchral brasses', *Publications of the Cambridge Antiquarian Society*, XIV (1847), 1–5. Idem, 'The genealogical history of the Freville family, with some account of their monuments in Little Shelford Church, Cambridgeshire', Ibid., 21–9.
17. A.W. Franks, *A Book of Ornamental Glazing Quarries*, London/Oxford 1849.
18. [A.W. Franks], *Catalogue of Works of Ancient and Medieval Art Exhibited at the House of the Society of Arts*, London 1850.
19. *Report of the Commissioners appointed to Inquire into the Constitution and Government of the British Museum*, 1850, 38ff. British Museum Standing Committee Minutes 1850, 8006, 8091; British Museum General Meeting

Minutes 14 Dec. 1850, 2111.
20 *Apology*, 3f.
21 British Museum Standing Committee Minutes 14 June 1851, 8227.
22 J. Evans, *A History of the Society of Antiquaries*, London 1956, 293ff.
23 British Museum Standing Committee Minutes 11 July 1857/1 Aug. 1857, 9241 and 9257.
24 *Report from the Select Committee on the British Museum* (Parliamentary Papers, House of Commons) 1860, xvi, 173, para. 18.
25 Birch to Franks 2.xii.61. British Museum Archives, BM. WAA (ANTS) corres.
26 Franks to Coxe 1863. British Museum Archives, BM. WAA (ANTS) corres.
27 Information from Mr T. Mitchell.
28 J.M. Kemble, *Horae Ferales; or, Studies in the archaeology of the Northern nations*, London 1863.
29 Society of Antiquaries MS 862.
30 J.M. de Navarro, 'A Survey of research on an early phase of Celtic Culture', *Proceedings of the British Academy*, xxii (1936), 11f.
31 *Archaeologia* xxxix (1863).
32 E. Hawkins, *Medallic Illustrations* ... (ed. A.W. Franks and H.A. Grueber), London 1885.
33 C.E. Schreiber, *Playing Cards of Various Ages* (ed. A.W. Franks), London 1892-5.
34 A.W. Franks, *Guide to the Christy Collection* ..., London 1868.
35 A. W. Franks, 'Notes on the discovery of stone implements in Japan', *International Congress of Prehistoric Archaeology: Transactions* ..., London 1869, 258-66.
36 A.W. Franks, 'Sur la composition des instruments en métal trouvés dans l'Ile de Chypre ...', *Congrès international d'anthropologie et d'archéologie préhistoriques, compte rendue* ..., iii, Stockholm 1876, 346-51.
37 G.E. Daniel, *A Hundred Years of Archaeology*, London 1950, 98.
38 G.F. Browne, *The Recollections of a Bishop*, London 1915, 209.
39 *Apology*, 21
40 British Museum Archives, BM. WAA (ANTS) Corres., 2203.
41 British Museum Officers' Reports, liv (Jan.-May 1855).
42 British Museum Archives, BM. WAA (ANTS) Corres., 2221 (6 March 1855).
43 B. Faussett, *Inventorium sepulchrale*, London 1856 v-vi.
44 British Museum Officers' Reports, liv (Jan.-May 1855), 10/2/55.
45 D. Kidd, 'Charles Roach-Smith and his Museum of London Antiquities', *Collectors and Collections*, London 1977 (The British Museum Yearbook 2), 105-36.
46 J. Evans, *Time and Chance* ..., London 1943, 102.
47 F.E. Barth and F.R. Hodson, 'The Hallstatt cemetery and its documentation: some new evidence', *The Antiquaries Journal*, lvi (1977), 175.
48 *West Yorkshire Archaeological Survey to A.D. 1500*, 1981, i, 188.
49 D.M. Wilson, *Anglo-Saxon Ornamental Metalwork, 700-1100, in the British Museum*, London

1964, 118f.
50 Henry Christy, A Pioneer of Anthropology, The British Museum, London 1965.
51 Apology, 7.
52 Ibid., 14.
53 Ibid., 15f.
54 C.H. Read and A.B. Tonnochy, Catalogue of the Silver Plate..., London 1928.
55 O.M. Dalton, Catalogue of the Finger-Rings, Early Christian..., London 1912; cf. also F.H. Maxwell, Catalogue of Finger-Rings, Greek, Etruscan and Roman..., London 1907.
56 O.M. Dalton, The Treasure of the Oxus..., London 1926.
57 E.R.J. Gambier Howe, Catalogue of British and American Book Plates..., London 1903.
58 D.M. Wilson and C.E. Blunt, 'The Trewhiddle Hoard', Archaeologia xcviii, 75n.
59 Apology, 1.
60 Lund, University Library MS. Saml. Nilsson, S. 6 Dec. 1868.
61 Twenty-five Years of the National Art-Collections Fund, Glasgow 1928, 3.
62 M. Wheeler, Still Digging, abridged ed., London 1958, 31f.

ACKNOWLEDGMENTS

In writing this small book I have been most grateful to many colleagues in the British Museum who have answered questions and provided photographs with great patience. I must also thank Miss F. Wright for graciously allowing me to use unpublished manuscripts belonging to the Franks family. My particular gratitude goes to Marjorie Caygill who did a considerable amount of work on the history of the Franks family and who generally bore the heat of the day.

I wish to acknowledge the permission of the Trustees of the British Museum for the publication of all the plates except Pl. 1 (Dr D. Roe), Pl. 6 (*Illustrated London News*), Pl. 35 (Trustees of the National Gallery) and Pl. 39 (D. M. Wilson).